Reptile Keeper's Guides

GARTER AND RIBBON SNAKES

R.D. Bartlett
Patricia Bartlett

BARRON'S

Acknowledgments

Rob MacInnes, Mike Stuhlman, and Chuck Hurt of Glades Herp, Inc., Chris McQuade of Gulf Coast Reptiles, and Craig McIntyre provided specimens and photographic opportunities. Paul Hollander and Phil Blais, M.D., have generously allowed us use of photos. Kenny Wray, Ron Sayers, Gus Rentfro, Denny Miller, Scott Cushnir, Chris Bednarski, and Courtney Watkins have accompanied us in our searches for these interesting and beautiful snakes. Scott Felzer shared his knowledge with us. We'd also like to thank the dedicated hobbyists and professional herpetologists who have shared their observations about garter snakes with us. Dave Schleser thoughtfully evaluated the initial manuscript. To all, and to our editor Pat Hunter, we offer our sincerest thanks.

All inquiries should be addressed to:
Barron's Educational Series, Inc.
250 Wireless Boulevard
Hauppauge, NY 11788
http://www.barronseduc.com

International Standard Book No. 0-7641-1698-3

Library of Congress Catalog Card No. 2001025255

Library of Congress Cataloging-in-Publication Data
Bartlett, Richard D., 1938–
     Garter and ribbon snakes : facts & advice on care and breeding / R. D. Bartlett and Patricia Bartlett.
       p. cm. — (Reptile keeper's guide)
    ISBN 0-7641-1698-3
     1. Garter snakes. 2. Snakes as pets. I. Bartlett, Patricia Pope, 1949– . II. Title.
SF459.S5 B372   2001
639.3′96—dc21   2001025255

Printed in Hong Kong
9 8 7 6 5 4 3 2 1

Contents

Preface
2

Introduction
3

**What Are the Garter Snakes
and Ribbon Snakes?**
5

**Garter Snakes and
Ribbon Snakes as Pets**
13

Caging
19

Feeding
27

Health
30

Colors
35

Breeding
39

Special Interest Groups
43

Glossary
44

Index
46

Preface

The garter snakes and the ribbon snakes (which are simply slender garter snakes) have long been among the most favored snakes of European hobbyists. There they sell for high prices and are eagerly sought. Despite the fact that they are indigenous to the Americas, it is only recently that these beautiful snakes have become popular with American hobbyists. The garter and ribbon snakes are restricted in distribution to North and Middle America. Some species, in some areas, are among the most common of snakes.

As garter snakes have become more popular pets, and have been bred in increasing numbers, new color morphs have spontaneously appeared. Of these, several, such as the flame and the albino phases of the eastern garter snake, and the albino phase of both the Plains and the checkered garter snakes, are now firmly established and available each year in at least small numbers. Like all "limited editions," the price for these aberrancies is considerably higher than the price of normally colored garter snakes.

Garter snakes are among the most ideal snakes for beginning hobbyists. They are nonvenomous, fairly small, not awfully hard to handle, prettily colored, very hardy, affordable, and very readily obtainable. In fact, because many of the species remain common in suburban settings, garter snakes are usually among the first snake species with which city dwellers become familiar. They are live-bearing snakes that often have large litters. In fact, the record clutch for one of the eastern garter snakes contained 85 babies. The neonates are almost identical in coloration to the adults.

The most widely ranging form, the eastern garter snake, *Thamnophis sirtalis,* is found in one subspecies or another from the Atlantic coast to the Pacific coast to the Gulf coast, and ranges northward to central Canada.

With their burgeoning popularity in herpetoculture has come a greater need for in-depth knowledge of these backyard snakes. It was with this in mind that we prepared this book.

A portrait of a western ribbon snake.

Introduction

In the eastern United States, garter snakes are synonymous with striping. So are the ribbon snakes, which are slender, wetland-dwelling garter snakes. In the American West however, things are a little different. There, depending on the species and subspecies, garter snakes can be either striped or blotched, and there are no ribbon snakes at all.

But no matter where they are from, the garter and ribbon snakes are often the snakes with which folks first become acquainted. This is because garter snakes of one form or another are snakes that adapt well to urban and suburban areas. They are not demanding in terms of food or shelter. Because of their catholic feeding habits and ability to utilize even the smallest piece of debris as shelter, garter snakes are among the few snake species able to coexist with humans. For many of us, our first snake memories are of finding garter snakes lying under a board in the garden, resting underwater in a tiny stream, or cruising among the grasses at a pond's edge.

Garter snakes do not find it easy to coexist with us, for humans often do not tolerate the presence of snakes well—even nonvenomous species that max out at 42 inches (105 cm) and consume tadpoles and earthworms.

But wherever they are not purposely persecuted (and sometimes even where they are), in many areas of our country garter snakes continue to be found easily in dooryards, vacant fields, fencerows, gardens, and commercial agricultural areas. Where irrigation canals or drainage ditches draw frogs and toads, these colorful snakes may be actually abundant. If you're really lucky out in the field, you may locate that ideal discarded mattress or roofing tin, which in turn shelters a dozen or so garters.

In coloration, garter snakes range from the mundane to the magnificent. They vary when adult from small to moderately sized. Captive garter snakes require little in the way of support materials, and usually thrive (but

This is a prowling San Francisco garter snake.

The broad, deep yellow vertebral stripe is characteristic of the coastal garter snake, *T.elegans terrestris.*

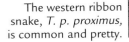

The western ribbon snake, *T. p. proximus,* is common and pretty.

may not breed) if kept year round at room temperature and illuminated from above with a small incandescent bulb. The fact that these snakes do not require mice in their diet makes them of interest to hobbyists who prefer not to feed snakes endotherms.

To list their drawbacks, garter snakes are secretive, sometimes flighty, may musk on the hand that holds them, and the occasional one may bite if suddenly grasped. However, with just a little keeper training, all of these minor adversities can be overcome, and you will be able to enjoy these beautiful, hardy, and long-lived snakes.

In this book we discuss the keeping of some of the most popular species of garter snakes that are readily available north of the Mexican border. We have made no effort to list several seldom seen American forms, and since the Mexican forms are virtually unknown in herpetoculture, we have not made mention of them.

We hope you will be encouraged to keep garter snakes, if you don't already, and that you will find this book useful in your endeavors.

A portrait of a juvenile Baja garter snake.

What Are the Garter Snakes and Ribbon Snakes?

The garter snakes and the water snakes comprise the subfamily Natricinae in the very large family of Colubridae. All of the garter snakes are in the genus *Thamnophis*. Of the 30 species, 16 (including two slender species called ribbon snakes) occur in the United States. This certainly gives a dedicated herpetoculturist enough variety to fill a room with cages. To add to the variety, many of these genera are subspeciated. In fact, the common garter snake, *T. s. sirtalis*, is represented from coast to coast to coast by 12 subspecies. All garter snakes have keeled scales.

Unlike the black, yellow, and red rat snakes, garter snakes can be remarkably hard to identify to species. They all look basically alike. Geographic origin, the scale rows on which the lateral stripes occur, whether these stripes are straight edged or wavy, along with head color, are important factors in garter snake identification. For many people, it makes the process of identifying a garter snake a bit tedious.

All garter snakes are of moderate size—18 inches to about 42 inches (45 to 105 cm). They are ovoviviparous, having large litters of live young.

A portrait of a flame morph garter snake. Photo by Phil Blais, M.D.

Garter snakes and ribbon snakes are found in the proximity of water, but some garters range long distances away from this medium. They seem to like grasslands, and debris under which they hide.

Species and Subspecies of American Garter Snakes

In one or another of its 12 subspecies, the eastern garter snake, *T. s. sirtalis*, is one of the world's most widely distributed and adaptive snakes. It is a snake

The red belly outlined with black dots separates the related Kirtland's snake, *Clonophis kirtlandi,* from the garter snakes.

Only the lined snake, *Tropidoclonion lineatum,* has two lines of black half-moons on the belly and yellow(ish) dorsal stripes. It is related to, but is not, a garter snake.

that most Americans recognize. It may be found in suitable habitats from the seaside dunes of the Atlantic Ocean to the seaside cliffs of the Pacific. It occurs from coast to coast in southern Canada, and from the southernmost tip of the Florida peninsula to just a few miles north of the U.S./Mexican border in California. The eastern garter snake is, however, absent from the American southwest where it is replaced by aridland species. The eastern garter snake is also absent from a vast area of northern Montana, southern Saskatchewan and southern Alberta. Over most of that area it is replaced by the Plains, *T. radix,* and wandering, *T. elegans,* garter snakes.

The eastern garter snake, *Thamnophis s. sirtalis,* is among the most variably colored of all the sub-species of the common garter snake. Typically it is a black(ish) snake boldly patterned with three longitudinal yellow stripes. However, the ground color may vary from olive through gray to tan and stripes from tan to bluish. In some populations the stripes are lacking (or poorly defined) and a checkerboard pattern is present. Melanistic specimens,

entirely black except for a few white chin-scales, are commonly encountered in the Great Lakes Region. Albino specimens are fairly common.

The blue-striped garter snake, *T. s. similis,* is restricted in distribution to the coastal areas of Florida's "Big Bend." This is a very poorly differentiated subspecies, for blue-striped individuals of the eastern garter snake are well known from the Florida peninsula as well.

The red-spotted garter snake, *Thamnophis s. concinnus,* is a subspecies of coastal northwestern Oregon and southwestern Washington. The ground color is ebony. Spots, which may vary from vermilion to butter yellow, are present on the sides, and the yellow vertebral stripe is well defined. There are no lateral stripes. The top of the head is usually red.

To the north of the range of the red-spotted garter snake one encounters the Puget Sound garter, *T. s. pickeringi*. Although often thought of as a "red-sided" garter snake, some are just yellow and black. The top of the head is dark.

In its ever-dwindling habitat on the western San Francisco peninsula of central California one may still find a few of one of the world's most beautiful snakes. This is the federally endangered San Francisco garter snake, *T. s. tetrataenia*. Although you *can* still sight them "in the wild," the penalties for harassing or collecting these snakes are harsh. The San Francisco garter snake is typified by a solid fire-orange to red-orange dorsolateral stripe along each side. Only a few of these snakes are in private collections in the United States or Europe. Some zoos do breed them, but federal regulations on endangered species can make finding homes for the offspring at the least difficult and at the worst, red-tape-laden. The Endangered Species Act

The Plains garter snake, *T. radix*, ranges widely in the plains states of the United States and southern Canada.

prevents captive breeding by private owners unless a permit is obtained.

The red-sided garter snake, *T. s. parietalis*, is a common but variably colored race of the plains and northwestern states. The pattern may vary from discrete red bars extending upwards from a well-defined lateral stripe, to some having the red extending in checkerboard-like squares from

As demonstrated by this coastal garter snake, *T. elegans terrestris,* red is not an uncommon coloration in several species of garter snakes.

(Left) The red-sided garter snake, *T. sirtalis parietalis,* typically bears much red in its color scheme.

The eastern black-necked garter snake is brightly colored and precisely patterned.

lateral to dorsal stripe, while others may lack much of the red. The head of this race is black.

In distribution, the New Mexico garter snake, *T. s. dorsalis,* is restricted to the Rio Grande Valley of the state from which it takes its name. In appearance it is much like a very dull common red-sided garter.

The Texas garter snake, *T. s. annectens,* lacks red on the sides; it bears a broad and intensely orange vertebral stripe. It is found in two disjunct populations: one in east-central Texas and the other in northeast Texas and western Oklahoma (but not on the Oklahoma panhandle).

The Chicago garter snake, *T. s. semifasciatus* is very similar to the eastern, differing principally in having the anterior lateral stripe interrupted by a half dozen (or so) black bars.

The Maritime garter snake, *T. s. pallidulus,* is a dull and obscurely marked race from northern New England and eastern Canada.

The Valley garter snake, *T. s. fitchi,* has some red on the sides and prominent lateral and middorsal stripes are prominent. The Valley garter snake occurs from extreme southern Alaska (the only snake to be found in that state) through western

Canada to Nevada and central California. The California red-sided (sometimes called the California red-spotted) garter snake, *T. s. infernalis,* is a pretty race that ranges over much of coastal California. It is a red-sided form that has poorly defined lateral stripes and a red head.

The Plains garter snake, *Thamnophis radix,* is usually both prominently striped and checkered. The lateral stripes occur on the third and fourth scale rows above the ventral scutes. Albinos have been found.

Two easily confused garter snake species exist in south-central and southwestern United States, from whence they range far southward into Latin America. These are the black-necked garter snakes, *T. cyrtopsis* ssp., and the checkered, *T. marcianus* ssp.

The eastern black-necked garter snake, *T. cyrtopsis ocellatus,* is one of the most beautiful of American thamnophines. The ground color is olive, and there is a large black blotch (contiguous with the dark of the top of the head) on each side of the neck. The vertebral stripe is orange, the lateral stripes are lacking. Anteriorly, the black lateral blotches are large, discrete, encroach upon, and cause the vertebral stripe to appear wavy. Posteriorly, the dark spots coalesce, forming a continuous, wide, black band along the upper side. A series of small, discrete, ventrolateral spots begins on the neck and continues for nearly the entire length of the snake's body.

The western subspecies of this snake, *T. c. cyrtopsis*, is less precisely marked (in fact it can be easily mistaken for a checkered garter snake) and although not brilliantly colored, the lateral stripes are usually evident.

Both the checkered and the black-necked garter snake have checkerboard patterns and dark blotches immediately behind the head. The neck blotches of the checkered garter are often proportionately larger and more posteriorly directed than the more rounded ones of the black-neck.

Perhaps the most definitive characteristic between the checkered and the black-necked garter snakes (as well as the one most difficult to ascertain) is scale row count. The checkered garter snake has midbody scale row count of 21; those of the black-necked garter snake are arranged in 19 rows. The scale row(s) on which the lateral stripes occur may also help determine the species. The lateral stripe of the checkered garter snake is restricted to a single row of scales (the

third row above the ventral plates) anteriorly, but involves the second and third rows posteriorly. The lateral stripe of the western black-necked garter snake, *T. c. cyrtopsis*, involves rows 2 and 3 for its entire length. Because of the staggered arrangement of the anteriolateral dark blotches, the position of the lateral stripe of the eastern black-necked garter snake, *T. c. ocellatus*, is usually difficult to define, at least anteriorly.

Not all garter snakes have a prominent middorsal stripe. For instance, the two-striped garter, *T. hammondi*, entirely lacks a vertebral stripe. This olive-drab snake usually has lateral stripes and these may, or may not, be bordered by black spots. It is found from Monterey Bay, California southward to northern Baja.

North of Monterey Bay (to San Francisco Bay) one may encounter the very pretty Santa Cruz garter snake, *T. atratus*. The Santa Cruz garter snake has a broad, precisely delineated vertebral stripe, but may lack the lateral stripes.

The narrow-headed garter snake, *T. rufipunctatus*, looks and acts more like a water snake, than a garter snake. This inhabitant of the mountains of central Arizona and New Mexico, and

Compared with its eastern subspecies, the western black-necked garter snake, *T. c. cyrtopsis,* is rather dull in color.

The peninsula ribbon snake, *T. sauritus sackenii,* is the most pallid of the eastern races in coloration.

This brightly colored Santa Cruz garter snake, *T. a. atratus,* is in a defensive posture.

northern Mexico, is of a dingy olive ground color with narrow middorsal blotches and alternating lateral spots. The eyes are situated high on the sides of the rather narrow head. It attains a length of 30 inches (75 cm).

The pretty and variable northwestern garter snake, *T. ordinoides,* is common from northern California to Vancouver Island and adjacent mainland British Columbia, Canada. The ground color may be tan, brown, or black and the middorsal stripe blue, orange, or yellow. The lateral stripes are often absent. Although exceptional specimens may exceed 3 feet (.9 m) in total length, between 20 and 24 inches (50 and 60 cm) is the more common adult size.

Butler's garter snake, *T. butleri,* of Wisconsin, Michigan, Ohio, and Indiana seldom exceeds two feet (.6 m) in length. The very similar appearing short-headed garter snake, *T. brachy-*stoma, of New York and Pennsylvania, is even smaller. Both are brown to near-black with buff to yellow stripes.

At 20 to 30 inches (50 to 75 cm) in length, all are of moderate size. *T. e. vagrans,* the wandering garter snake, is a pallid colored, but immensely hardy, form that ranges widely in the American West. Those from the southernmost portion of its range have recently been assigned to the new race, *T. e. arizonae* (Arizona garter snake), and those from eastern Utah to *T. e. vascotanneri* (Upper Basin garter snake). *T. e. terrestris,* the coast garter snake, occurs in two very different morphs. One is a typical yellow striped black phase, but the other bears yellow stripes, black, checkers, and an orange-red ground color.

There are but two species (8 subspecies) of ribbon snakes (*T. sauritus* ssp. and *T. proximus* ssp.). Most are adult at 30 inches (75 cm) or less.

The largest size recorded for the largest subspecies, the aridland ribbon snake, is only 48.5 inches (121.25 cm). Of the ribbon snake's total length, about a third is tail.

Both species of ribbon snake are of very similar appearance. On all (the sole possible exception being the Peninsula ribbon snake, *T. sauritus sackenii,* which may have the vertebral stripe reduced or absent) the stripes are precisely delineated. The eastern species has a dark ventrolateral stripe, which involves the outermost tips of the ventral plates. Although present on the western species, the ventrolateral stripe is usually narrower, less well defined and restricted to the body scales.

The eastern ribbon snake shows a tendency for north to south differences in color and pattern intensity. The darkest race is the northern ribbon snake, *T. sauritus septentrionalis,* of southern Quebec and Ontario to southern Maine, New York, central Ohio and southern Indiana. The stripes are yellow-ochre or brownish-yellow against a jet black dorsal color.

The eastern ribbon snake, *T. s. sauritus,* occurs in a big, unequal

A freshly shed Butler's garter snake, *T. butleri.*

sided "U" southward from southern Maine and central-eastern New York, through all of the Atlantic coastal states to the Gulf. It then ranges westward to eastern Louisiana and northward to the Mississippi River Valley to southern Illinois and Indiana. The ground color varies from dark tan through olive-brown to nearly black. The lateral lines are yellow and the middorsal stripe may vary from yellow to bluish-green or orange.

The Peninsula ribbon snake, *T. sauritus sackenii,* is the southernmost and the palest race. It is restricted in distribution to the Florida peninsula,

The common name of short-headed garter snake, *T. brachystoma,* accurately portrays a characteristic of the species.

southeast Georgia and extreme southeast South Carolina. Its scales often appear dusty with the markings not in strong contrast. Melanism is known to occur in this race.

The blue-striped, *T. sauritus nitae,* is found only along Florida's Big Bend. The ground color is dark (often black) and the stripes are bright to pale blue.

Of the four subspecies of the western ribbon snake, only the nominate, the western, *T. p. proximus,* is offered for sale with any degree of regularity. It has large, well-defined parietal spots and an orange vertebral line against a black ground color. It ranges widely from the latitude of central

Louisiana and Texas, northward to southern Iowa and southwestern Wisconsin.

Three races have an olive-brown to grayish ground color. The common name defines the pretty red-striped ribbon snake, *T. p. rubrilineatus,* of central Texas. Albinism has been reported in both this and the western ribbon snakes. The aridland ribbon snake, *T. p. diabolicus,* has an orange vertebral stripe. It ranges from the Mexican state of Nuevo Leon, north to northern New Mexico. The Gulf Coast ribbon snake, *T. p. orarius,* has a gold vertebral stripe and is found in coastal drainages from Louisiana to the Lower Rio Grande Valley.

The red-striped ribbon snake, *T. proximus rubrilineatus,* has an intensely colored vertebral stripe.

The blue-striped ribbon snake, *T. sauritus nitae,* is typified by bluish-white striping.

Garter Snakes and Ribbon Snakes as Pets

Garter snakes and ribbon snakes have long been favorites of the herpetocultural community. They are considered ideal, sturdy, beginner's snakes. They are not demanding, are too small to do much damage should they decide to bite, and are easy to feed. (Ease of feeding really hits home if you're trying to find crayfish in the dead of winter for one of the crayfish snakes.) Unlike their relatives the water snakes, garter snakes are also pretty enough to maintain interest.

Although garter snakes may at first resist familiarity by flattening their head and striking savagely (ribbon snakes are more apt to just try to flee), they quickly become accustomed to handling. Although it's unsettling to be bitten by a garter snake even once, they do calm down. Most of those seen in the pet trade are of small to moderate size, but some can grow to a good size of just under 4 feet (1.2 m) as adults.

Although they are comparatively small as adults, you must take the snake's maximum size into consideration when determining terrarium size. To generalize, you can keep three or four 7-inch (17.5-cm) long neonate garter snakes in a 10-gallon (38-L) terrarium, but we suggest that for the same number of adults you use a 40-gallon (152-L) capacity, or larger.

Because of their high metabolism and low fat diet, captive garter snakes must be fed frequently. They have healthy appetites, and are ready to repeat the feeding process every day or two. They stool often, a factor that translates to frequent cage cleaning. They will enjoy a sizable water dish in which to submerge and bask.

These active snakes display periods of intense, almost nervous,

The four rows of teeth can be seen in the upper jaw of this blue-striped garter snake, *T. sirtalis similis*.

activity. They often slide repeatedly through, and in and out of the water, thoroughly dampening their cage. This is where the cage set-up counts. It is important that the cage dry quickly. Dampness can cause skin infections, which, if unchecked, look terrible and can become lethal. Set your cage up so keeping it dry won't be much work. (You still have to go out and dig/buy enough earthworms to keep your snakes well-fed.) Try to cut down on the work involved in keeping your cages clean and problem-free. We suggest a substrate of either folded newspaper or a carpet of fallen oak leaves. Both are readily available and easily changed and discarded. Water tends to go to the bottom layer of the newspaper or the leaves, and the top layers tend to be slightly drier.

Not all garter snakes are equally popular as pets. What determines why one kind of garter snake is popular while another is not? As with other colubrine snakes, hobbyists tend to keep greater numbers of those that are either very common and hence easily acquired (often found on afternoon family strolls or by exploring children), very rare (a certain mystique often accompanies the keeping of an uncommonly seen snake—don't be tempted by endangered forms though!), of an unusual color (albinos, and so on), or very pretty.

The garter snakes most often seen in captivity are normal, melanistic, albino, and flame morphs of the eastern garter snake. Besides these, normally colored phases of the red-spotted and red-sided garter snakes, albino and normal plains garter snakes, and albino and normal checkered garter snakes are seen commonly as captives. Other favorites are eastern black-necked garter snakes, the red morph of the coast garter snake, and the brighter examples of the California red-sided garter snake. All are pretty and all are easily kept.

Collecting Your Garter Snake from the Wild

Like all snakes, garter snakes are pretty much where you find them, but you can enhance your chances by looking in certain habitats.

A portrait of a blue-striped garter snake.

This blue-striped garter snake came from well east of the described range for this race.

Some State-Protected Garter Snakes

The listings of protected reptiles are continually under review and frequently changed. We urge you to keep current.

State	Protected Species/Subspecies
California	Giant Garter Snake
California	Two-striped Garter Snake
California	San Francisco Garter Snake*
Florida	Peninsula Ribbon Snake (Florida Keys populations)
Illinois	Ribbon Snake (all subspecies)
Indiana	Butler's Garter Snake
Kansas	Checkered Garter Snake
New Mexico	Northern Mexican Garter Snake
New Mexico	Aridland Ribbon Snake
New Mexico	Narrow-headed Garter Snake
Ohio	Plains Garter Snake
Wisconsin	Western Ribbon Snake
Wisconsin	Northern Ribbon Snake

*Also federally protected

However, before you rush out to collect your own garter snake from the wild, check the legalities of doing so with the non-game division of your state game and fish department. Several species and subspecies are protected by law in the states in which they occur and, in addition, the San Francisco garter snake is federally protected.

Both the garter and the ribbon snakes are secretive species. Although they may be out and foraging by day if hungry, or basking in the spring sunshine, these snakes usually rest quietly beneath surface debris.

You may happen across a garter snake or a ribbon snake on a wooded trail or along a weedy inlet of your favorite fishing hole, but you will often have to actually search to find one of these snakes. Be sure you learn

The beautiful San Francisco garter snake, *T. sirtalis tetrataenia,* is an endangered form.

The narrow-headed garter snake, *T. rufipunctatus,* is a southwestern species that looks and acts more like a water snake.

A portrait of a narrow-headed garter snake.

by sight all of the venomous snakes in the area you are planning to hunt; venomous and nonvenomous species may share the same resting spot. Unless they have aberrant patterns, there are no striped venomous species in the United States, but some of the blotched or saddled garter snakes may confuse a novice seeker.

Look for garter snakes by turning over pieces of cardboard, plywood, roofing tin, or other such human-generated debris. Once uncovered, be ready to grab the snake firmly but *gently,* and to do so quickly for often, once disturbed, a garter snake will move off very rapidly.

As they prepare to shed their skin, garter snakes hide persistently. At this time vision is impaired, and the scales can be damaged if the skin is torn. These, and all snakes, are then at their most vulnerable. This is one reason for grasping the snake gently.

Purchasing Your Garter Snake

Collecting your own garter snakes is an excellent way of obtaining snakes indigenous to your area, or of even picking up a specimen or two from some distant region you happen to be visiting. But there are also other ways of getting a garter snake.

Pet stores may offer exotic species or specialist reptile dealers may have types that would not be otherwise available to you. There are a few breeders of garter snakes who sell their captive-born garter snake babies, and reptile expos are a particularly good source of some eagerly sought species. Peruse the ads in reptile hobbyist magazines, and search the Internet for garter snakes or ribbon snakes.

Quite often, when you do find what you are looking for, it will be a dealer a fair distance from where you are located. How, then, do you go about getting the snake you have chosen?

Ordering and Shipping

From airports in the larger cities, reptiles are air-freighted to both pet shops and individuals. When contemplating having a garter snake shipped to you, you must think about the shipping charges. Depending upon the complexity involved in getting an air shipment from the point of origin to the airport closest to you, or your home (the choice will probably be yours) shipping costs may vary from about $25 to close to $80.

You may be asked to pay for the animal and the shipping charges in advance. Your shipper will need your credit card number and expiration date, a money order, or a cashier's check. Many shippers will accept personal checks but will wait until the check clears the bank before shipping (usually within a week or so).

COD service may be available, but it usually adds even more charges to the cost of shipping, and some companies will accept only cash for the charges.

Your supplier will need your full name, address, and current day and evening telephone numbers. Inform your shipper of the airport you wish to use, or agree on a door-to-door delivery company. If your area is serviced by more than one airport (such as the Washington, DC or San Francisco, California areas) be very specific about which airport you expect to find your shipment.

Agree on a shipping date and on that date call your supplier for the air-bill number. Some shippers go to the

Eastern garter snakes are often found prowling amidst stumps and branches in damp woodlands.

The red-spotted garter snake, *T. sirtalis concinnus,* is a spectacular northwestern race of the eastern garter snake.

airport on only one or two specific days each week. Avoid weekend arrivals when the cargo offices at most small airports are closed.

Most shipments take about 24 hours to get from the airport of origin to the airport of destination. Keep your shipment on the same airline whenever possible; with live animals you pay for each airline involved. Ship only during "good" weather. Your snake may be delayed when the weather is very hot, very cold, or during the peak holiday travel/shipping/mailing times.

The overnight, door-to-door services of companies such as Federal Express, UPS, or Airborne Express may be available for shipping reptiles. Check with your supplier.

After a reasonable time, call the airline that your shipment is traveling on and ask them for the status of the shipment. The airline will need the airbill number to trace the shipment in their computer.

Once it has arrived, claim your shipment as quickly as possible. This is especially important in bad weather. Learn the operating hours of your cargo office and whether the shipment can be picked up at the ticket counter if it arrives after the cargo office has closed.

After paying the applicable charges, open and inspect your shipment before leaving the cargo facility. Unless otherwise specified, reliable shippers guarantee live delivery. However, if there is a problem, both the shipper and the airline(s), will require a "discrepancy" or "damage" report made out, *signed and dated* by airline cargo personnel. In the very rare case when a problem has occurred, insist on the completion and filing of a claim form right then and contact your shipper immediately for instructions.

This may seem complex, but using air freight is a very simple and comparatively fast and safe way to ship snakes.

Caging

Although mention is often made of the cannibalistic tendencies of milk snakes and kingsnakes, seldom is this characteristic mentioned when garter snakes are discussed. Perhaps it is because less is known about the feeding habits of these natricines, or perhaps it is because many (including the ribbon snakes) are not cannibalistic, but since cannibalism has occurred more often than just occasionally, it is something that should be mentioned. Prevention is easy: Simply do not transport, feed, or house garter snakes of disparate sizes together. It seems probable that those species and subspecies of garter snakes that normally accept a wide variety of prey items (Plains garter snakes, wandering garter snakes, and so on) are more apt than specialized feeders to indulge in cannibalism, but take no chances. Do not mix sizes.

There is also a chance of cannibalism occurring at feeding time. If two garter snakes begin eating the opposite ends of the same earthworm, when the two meet in the middle, the larger or more aggressive feeder is apt to continue swallowing, consuming its cagemate. Watch your garter snakes carefully when feeding them.

Other than this possible problem, garter and ribbon snakes are relatively trouble-free snakes in captivity. They are easily cared for and housed. Their dietary staples of live minnows and earthworms (some forms do eat small rodents) are not difficult to obtain, and they require little in the way of UV emitting-lighting or supplementary vitamins and calcium.

Since these snakes do have a high metabolism, and since the dietary items they prefer are rather low in fats, they do require more frequent feeding than rodent-eating snakes. We suggest that babies be offered food at least three times weekly, and that adults be fed twice weekly. Fresh water and adequate caging are mandatory. These

Wandering garter snakes, *T. elegans vagrans,* are of subdued color and wide distribution.

19

snakes will thrive in spartan quarters with a minimum of 20 gallons (76 L).

The cage (including an earthen substrate if this is used) should be thoroughly cleaned and sterilized on a regular basis. There are excellent cleansing products available in most pet stores. A dilute solution of bleach can also be used safely. Do not clean cages with any solution containing pine oils, or other aromatic additives. Contact with, or breathing the fumes, may be toxic to the snakes.

As with most snake species, the garter and ribbon snakes are secretive by nature. To thrive as captives, they must feel secure. To feel secure, they will need suitable hiding areas. These can be in the form of simple hide boxes (called "hides" by most hobbyists), commercially manufactured hides, or other objects into or beneath which the snakes may retreat.

Cage furniture may consist of a growing plant, a plastic vine, a textured waterbowl/hide box combination, or any number of other single or combined items. The furniture should either be so light that if it shifts it cannot injure a snake coiled beneath it or, if heavy, should be adequately secured to prevent the snake from injuring itself. Garter snakes seem most comfortable if their hide is so small that their coiled body presses against both the sides and the top. They don't care whether this is a simple cut-to-size cardboard box, or commercial preformed plastic "caves" and combination cave water dishes. The former is very easily replaceable and the latter is washable, sterilizable, and will last for years. We provide natural hollow limbs and hollowed cactus skeletons that we find while out in woods and fields. Cactus skeletons (real or cast resin) are also commercially available.

Gently curved corkbark slabs and tightly curled corkbark tubes are lightweight alternatives to hollow limbs. Additionally, they are more impervious to body wastes, are easily cleaned, and can be sterilized for lengthy use. Corkbark is available at many pet stores, reptile dealers, and plant nurseries.

The prudent positioning of the hides will more or less dictate where in their cages the garter snakes will be. To view the snake, you need only to lift its hide box.

T. elegans vascotanneri derives its common name of Upper Basin garter snake from its distribution in the upper Great Basin region.

Secured rocks will also provide visual barriers and hiding areas for garter snakes. The keyword here is secured. Rocks, by definition, are heavy (except for lava rock, which we feel is too rough to be satisfactory) and, should they accidentally shift, may easily injure or kill your snake. If used against the back of the cage, rocks can be easily held in place with silicone aquarium sealant. If flat rocks are used as cage bottom hides, spacers of smaller rocks should be cemented in place to prevent them from settling on and crushing your snake.

This is the aridland race of the western ribbon snake, *T. proximus diabolicus*.

Your cage bottom substrate should be of a type that is easily cleaned or readily replaced. One that will allow your garter snakes to burrow and remain out of sight is ideal. Substrates consisting of a thick layer of nonaromatic mulch (cypress or aspen is ideal—cedar or strongly aromatic pine is not) or fallen leaves, are excellent burrowing media. Several layers of paper towels or newspaper are also easily replaced, readily available, inexpensive substrates. Unfortunately, the more satisfactory substrates often effectively obscure the ready viewing of the snake.

Fresh water should be provided in a low but fairly large dish. Both garter and ribbon snakes are strongly aquatic and may soak in their water for a day or two at a time. This is

The decidedly greenish hue of this eastern garter snake is unusual.

Found by Norm Damm, this unusual eastern garter snake has its colors reversed—a dark stripe against a light body color.

As their waterholes dry, aridland ribbon snakes must search diligently for a water source.

especially true if cage humidity is a little low or when the snake is entering its shedding cycle. These snakes often stool in their water bowl, necessitating immediate cleaning and sterilizing.

To shed properly, natricines require a fairly high cage humidity. Besides the water bowl, you may choose to provide your snakes with a covered plastic shoe box (with an

The Arizona garter snake, *T. elegans arizonae,* is a recently described form from central eastern Arizona and adjacent New Mexico.

access hole cut in the top) of barely dampened, unmilled sphagnum moss. Hiding in this will keep the snake's skin soft, pliable, and allow for easy shedding at the appropriate time.

Lighting and Heating the Cage

Like all snakes, garter and ribbon snakes are ectothermic creatures that regulate their body temperatures by utilizing outside sources of heating and cooling. They may warm themselves by choosing a secluded but sunny place and basking. Usually, especially when skin-shedding is imminent, they are more secretive, seeking warmth beneath sun-warmed ground surface litter.

Northern races hibernate, and even the southern forms may become dormant during the cooler, drier, shorter days of winter. At this time garters may refuse food and be persistently reclusive.

Effects of Photoperiod, Seasons, and Weather Patterns

It has long been known that photoperiod (day length versus night length), the changing seasons, and weather patterns affect the behavior of snakes. Of these three natural phenomena, the seasonal changes are the easiest to explain when dealing with snakes of temperate regions such as the garter snakes.

Snakes are ectotherms that must be relatively warm to operate efficiently. Since such temperatures are not attainable during temperate winters, garter and ribbon snakes hibernate. Coincidentally, the day lengths are the shortest during the winter months also.

As temperatures moderate in the spring of the year, cues (probably the rising temperatures) rouse the snakes from their (sometimes uneasy) slumber, and stimulate them to periods of activity that increase in duration as day temperatures warm through the spring and summer. Even before lowering temperatures are particularly noticeable in the autumn, diminishing photoperiods alert the reptiles to the need to begin the return to the wintering dens, and probably serve also to inform them that it's time to stoke up on the food necessary to tide them through another long winter.

That changing photoperiods are perceived by these snakes is apparent. Even if temperature and humidity are not altered from summer to winter, some snakes become lethargic during lengthy periods of reduced photoperiod, but regain normal activity (including breeding behavior) when photoperiods lengthen in the spring.

Naturally changing weather patterns—dry seasons, rainy seasons, low pressure frontal systems, the high pressure associated with fine weather,

even the lunar cycle—are known to affect snake behavior.

Garter snakes are most active during the passage of low pressure systems in the spring of the year. Those in the north emerge from hibernation and begin reproductive behavior almost immediately following emergence. They are especially active in the spring during the passage of frontal systems.

Caging Suggestions

The ability to thermoregulate is important for captive garter snakes. They, of course, are dependent on us, their keepers, to provide them with caging that permits them to select their optimum body temperature.

Albino checkered garter snakes are now regularly available in the pet marketplace.

This adult checkered garter snake was found on the Texas panhandle.

Garter snakes often hide beneath rocks and logs. This is an eastern garter snake.

Warming the cage may be done with under-cage heating pads and heating tapes, or with hot rocks because they have caused burns (these latter are not particularly recommended), or with above cage lighting.

Provide thermal gradients except during hibernation (see page 41), when the terrarium temperature should be uniformly cool. Normal night temperatures can be cooler by several degrees than daytime temperatures. In small tanks, we place the hide box on the cool end of the tank; if the tank is sufficiently large, we place a hide box on both ends.

Full-spectrum/ultraviolet lighting seems unnecessary for garter and ribbon snakes. Maintaining a proper cage humidity can be an important consideration in the successful maintenance of garter snakes. Species from humid areas will have shedding problems if the humidity is too low; species from arid areas can develop serious (even fatal) health problems if humidity is too high.

Besides serving as a drinking receptacle, the water bowl can play an integral part in raising or lowering the humidity in a cage. Cage humidity will be higher in a cage with less ventilation than in one with more.

If you wish to increase humidity in your cage, place a large water bowl in the hottest spot (over a heating pad if the latter is in use). If you wish to decrease, or keep humidity as low as possible, provide a small water dish and situate it in the coolest spot in the cage (the water dish should be large enough for the snake to coil in and soak).

More Thoughts on Caging

If sterility and absolute ease of maintenance is what you wish, your snake's cage can be very inexpensive.

Plastic shoe, sweater, and blanket boxes are often used and all are available in most hardware and department stores. Be sure the lids fit securely, or can be secured with tape or Velcro strips. Aquaria are somewhat more expensive, but are also readily available in pet and department stores throughout the world. Locking plastic or metal framed screen lids are a standard stock item.

If plastic caging is used, sufficient air (ventilation) holes must be drilled (or melted) through the sides to provide adequate air transfer and to prevent a buildup of humidity. We prefer ventilation on at least two sides and usually ventilate all four sides. If an aridland garter snake is being kept, we ventilate the top as well.

Cabinets that hold a dozen or more plastic boxes are now available, many with heat tapes built in. These are advertised in most reptile magazines and are available at many of the reptile meets.

Like all snakes, the thamnophines instinctively seem to find the weakest point in their caging, and will escape through seemingly impossible apertures. Cage them *securely*.

As long as they are fully secured with an escape-proof top, glass aquaria, oriented in the normal horizontal position, will serve well. Custom glass terraria can either be purchased or, if you are just the slightest bit handy, can be built by you. Merely take your measurements, cut the pieces of glass (or have them cut), and using a clear aquarium sealant, build your custom tank. The glass can be held in place with strips of tape while the sealant is curing (about 24 hours). The most important thing when using the sealant is to make absolutely certain that the edges of the glass that are to be sealed are entirely free of any oils or any other debris that could prevent the aquarium sealant from forming a tight seal. Remarkably large terraria can be held together very securely with aquarium sealant, especially if the tanks will not be intended to hold water.

A simplified combination of concepts can also be used. Our garter and ribbon snake terraria usually have a substrate of one or two inches (2.5 or

5 cm) of easily replaced dried leaves. (We use the very durable fallen leaves of the live oak, *Quercus virginianus,* when possible.) The water dishes are hidden behind logs gleaned from the woodlands and we usually have at least one thicket of potted, easily grown foliage plants (such as "pothos") for woodland species or rosettes of potted dwarf *Sansevieria* (*S. hahni* is among our favorites) for aridland species of garter snakes.

The Dry Savanna Terrarium

Even though many species and subspecies of garter snakes and both species of ribbon snakes come from naturally damp areas, it is better if they are kept dry in captivity. If you enjoy an aesthetically pleasing terrarium, we suggest that a dry savanna setup will be ideal.

To build one of these, begin with a 40-gallon (152-L) aquarium. We choose reptile tanks with escape-proof sliding screen tops. These have a thinner glass than a normal terrarium.

This eastern garter snake was basking on the stump of a tree in Ohio.

Eastern garter snakes may be very contrastingly colored, or pale, like this example.

Occasional incidents of piebald coloration are recorded in eastern garter snakes.

The glass will break if the tank is filled with water. However, they are less expensive than a typical aquarium.

The substrate should have 3 or 4 inches (7.5 or 10 cm) of sandy soil. Suitable water receptacle, plants, and hides can be added. (Cholla-cactus skeletons are ideal hides in this style tank.)

Plants for the Savanna Terrarium

The many species and cultivars of snakeplant or mother-in-law-tongue (genus *Sansevieria*) are ideal for brilliantly lighted savanna tanks. These are African plants that have been naturalized in many other areas of the world. Many are popular houseplants. The cultivars that form short, ground hugging rosettes are the best for garter snakes. The sansevierias are both hardy and drought tolerant. They can be propagated by offsets, by rooting leaf cuttings, and more rarely, by seed. As would be expected, the plants need more water during their periods of active growth than when they are dormant.

Cultivated species of purslane or portulaca are sold by nurseries for both hanging garden baskets and as bedding plants. They are drought tolerant succulents that are fragile and require very bright lighting. Because they are inexpensive and bear beautiful blossoms, these plants are occasionally used as expendable terrarium plants. Garter snakes will utilize these plants for cover.

Feeding

Although the ribbon snakes are more specialized than many of the garter snakes in their feeding preferences, collectively these thamnophines eat a very wide variety of animal matter. Most favored are minnows and tadpoles (ribbon snakes), earthworms (Butler's, northwestern, and short-headed garter snakes), or minnows, earthworms and an occasional frog (most other garter snakes). As a matter of fact, almost all amphibians—if they are small enough to be eaten—find favor with garter and ribbon snakes. They will also eat slugs, spiders, millipedes, and perhaps an occasional cricket. To this, you may add an occasional nestling mouse (a natural food for many of the western forms of garter snake, but one that most eastern forms of garter snakes must be enticed to eat). Babies of the smaller forms of garter and ribbon snakes may be so tiny that only small worms and the tiniest of fish can be swallowed.

You can try a commercial garter snake food or grub—there's at least one brand on the market. The food comes in a tiny can, and once out of the can it looks disconcertingly like

Some checkered garter snakes, *T. m. marcianus,* look very much like western black-necked garters.

those plump small smoked cocktail sausages served at evening parties, but this is food only for garter snakes. Offering these to your garter snake once a month or so not only makes feeding easy—should you suddenly have no earthworms or minnows, and only have a can of grub on the shelf—but if a non-snake person has to take care of your garter snake while you have major back surgery, that person will find feeding the grub a lot less distasteful than feeding worms or live fish.

Thawed frozen fish filets can be used as a stopgap food, but frozen filets are deficient in minerals and a number of vitamins, including thiamin. If you use frozen fish, you'll need to add a vitamin/mineral supplement that contains thiamin to the

diet. Whenever possible, offer frozen whole fish.

Almost any bait store fish can be substituted for minnows, as could "feeder" fish from your local pet store. Although goldfish have fallen out of favor as a major food item for most hobbyists, if your choice is between offering goldfish or nothing, offer the goldfish.

Because they are shy and secretive, these snakes may prefer to eat while under cover or while partially submerged in their water bowl. Place the food items on a flat rock, where the snake can see and smell them, or if you're offering live fish, put a couple into the water dish (more than one or two will deplete the oxygen in the water and all of the fish in the dish will die). If you have several garter snakes in a single cage, toss the earthworms into different corners of the cage so the snakes naturally separate to find their own earthworms.

A garter snake that finds another garter snake eating the end of "his" worm has sort of a "he's gotta let go first" attitude. You'd rather have two garter snakes than one really fat one. Feed them in separate areas so cannibalism doesn't happen.

The good news about garter snakes is that in the fall and early winter, just when the earthworms, tadpoles and minnows are harder to find yourself, the snakes will begin to eat less and less. Their appetite often naturally wanes with the approach of the shorter days of winter. This doesn't mean that you've done anything wrong.

You may try either or both of two things if your snake declines food in the winter. First, you can fuss with your snake, changing lighting, warmth, and feeding parameters, and hope that you hit on the combination that induces the snake to feed before the lengthening daylight hours of springtime automatically do so.

Earthworms are a favored food of many eastern garter snakes.

When they are distended with food, garter snakes (such as this baby flame garter snake) show patterns and colors not otherwise seen.

Second, if this doesn't work, you can cool the animal into a state of dormancy (see hibernation, page 41). In most cases, the cooling is the easier and more successful of the two.

When hungry, garter and ribbon snakes often prowl continually about their cage or sit with head extended from the hide box, alertly watching near-cage movements.

Scenting

The technique of scenting one prey type with the odor of another is a time-tested way to succeed in getting some snakes to accept dietary variety. Since many garter snakes refuse to eat mice, it is usually a mouse that their owner is trying to trick them into eating. To do so, scent a small, prekilled (and washed) mouse by rubbing a minnow against its nose. Slowly present the mouse to the snake in forceps or lay it in the opening of the snake's hide box. Your snake may accept the scented mouse on the first try (especially if the snake is hungry), or it may take several tries to entice it to do so. Ribbon snakes routinely refuse foods other than minnows, tadpoles, and occasionally, a tiny frog. Don't worry about this. Capitulate.

Remember that a varied and natural diet is best for your snake. Even if you do entice it to eat mice, do not make these the snake's exclusive diet.

Many wild-collected garter and ribbon snakes harbor substantial burdens of endoparasites. If overwhelming, this might cause your snake to be a reluctant eater, or to regurgitate after eating. The overall health of wild-collected snakes should be carefully monitored and a veterinary

---

Enticing Your Garter Snake to Eat

If your snake stops eating, here's what you can do:

- Ascertain that the hiding areas are still accessible.
- Elevate the cage temperature a little.
- Increase the cage humidity somewhat.
- Increase the daylight lighting intensity. The use of full-spectrum bulbs may help offset the effects of the lessened hours of daylight.
- Present the food very quietly, laying it nose first in the doorway of the snake's hide box.
- Try feeding the snake at different times of day and when its surroundings are absolutely quiet.
- If these all fail, try varying the kinds and sizes of prey.

---

assessment sought if necessary. Your veterinarian can easily tell from a stool sample whether a problem exists, and can provide effective treatment.

The Gulf Coast ribbon snake, *T. proximus orarius*, is a race of the western ribbon.

Health

Choosing a Healthy Garter Snake

It is not always easy to assess a snake's health. Select a garter snake that displays an alert demeanor but one that is not overly aggressive when it is disturbed. Select a snake that has good body weight—one that does not have folded, loose skin or "accordion" ribs. Actually see the snake eat, if possible.

A sneeze may indicate a respiratory infection (but could also indicate nothing more serious than clearing a few particles of dust from its nose); labored breathing may indicate a respiratory problem or could mean that lung flukes are present. If you feel uncertain about judging the health of a snake, seek the help of an experienced hobbyist when choosing your snake.

Shedding—What Is Normal?

A healthy, fast-growing baby garter snake will shed its skin several times a year. Larger specimens shed less frequently. Skin problems, such as blister disease (caused by unclean or overly damp caging), will accelerate a shedding cycle and can be fatal if not corrected.

Shedding (more properly termed ecdysis) results from thyroid activity. A week or so prior to shedding, as the old skin begins to loosen from the new one forming beneath it, your snake's pattern will dull and take on an overall grayish or silvery sheen. The snake's eyes will temporarily look bluish. A snake in this phase is colloquially referred to as "blue" or "opaque" by hobbyists, and may be quite irritable. Healthy snakes usually discard their skin in a single piece. Shedding problems can be caused by stress, dehydration, starvation, or when the relative humidity in the terrarium or cage is too low. Avoid shed-

This eastern garter snake lacks a light vertebral stripe.

ding problems by elevating relative humidity and occasionally misting a snake that is preparing to shed.

When ready to shed, your snake will loosen the skin along its lips by rubbing its nose and the sides of its face against a piece of cage furniture or the sides of its cage. The snake will then crawl slowly out of its old skin, inverting the shed as it emerges. It is important that no patches of old skin—especially eyecaps—remain attached to the snake. If the snake seems to have difficulty in the shedding process, place your snake in a damp cloth bag overnight (checking to be sure temperatures are suitable). Usually this will loosen the old skin and allow your snake to shed. You may have to occasionally manually help your snake rid itself of a particularly resistant shed. If patches of skin adhere, a gentle misting with tepid water, or a droplet of mineral oil, or of artificial tears, may help your snake rid itself of the pieces. Use tweezers and caution to remove old eyecaps, and don't hesitate to ask someone more experienced if you cannot tell if the old eyecaps are in place. After shedding, your specimen will again be as brightly hued and patterned as it was to begin with.

Quarantine

If you have more than one specimen, avoid the possible spread of diseases and parasites by quarantining new specimens. Keep the quarantine cage scrupulously clean by sterilizing it with a weak (1:10) Clorox solution. Wash your hands before going from cage to cage. A quarantine period of a month is suggested. During quarantine, observe your new snake frequently.

The haziness of this Butler's garter snake's eyes is due to an impending shed.

Watch for the usual danger signs—external parasites, labored breathing, sneezing, or abnormal stools. Have a veterinarian perform a fecal examination before you place the new specimen with those already being maintained. The quarantine area should be completely removed from the area in which other reptiles are kept, preferably in another room.

Ectoparasites

Ticks: Wild-collected garter snakes may bear ticks, and snake mites can plague collections. Ticks are the easier to deal with because they are bigger, present in only small concentrations, and are readily seen and removed. To remove a tick, very carefully coat it first with Vaseline or dab it with alcohol. (Use a cotton swab if you don't want to use your fingers.) After 10 to 20 minutes, the tick's grip will loosen, and you can remove it. Check that the sucking mouth parts are removed intact, and crush the arachnid before disposing of it.

This typically colored eastern garter snake is in a defensive pose.

Mites: These can be a recurring and persistent problem. A snake with mites may rub its face and body against its caging in an effort to dislodge the parasite. Mites appear as tiny dots near the eyes or under the belly scales. The belly scales may puff up and appear inflamed. A pervasive airborne insecticide, such as that contained in a "no-pest-strip," was once the combatant of choice, but an

Thamnophis ordinoides is referred to as the northwestern garter snake.

Ivermectin spray is now finding favor. Consult your veterinarian.

Burns and Abscesses

Prevention of these problems requires just a little forethought on the part of the keeper.

Burns: Keep all heat-emitting implements out of reach of the snake. Make sure the surface of your hot rocks or blocks do not go above 95°F (35°C). If your snake sustains burns through your carelessness or through carelessness on the part of someone else, the snake will need medical treatment. Cool the burned area and apply a clean, dry dressing, and take the snake to a veterinarian as quickly as possible.

Abscesses: An improperly sterilized and healed burn, cut, or bite may result in the formation of an abscess. Some eventually will heal and slough off or be rubbed off; a very few may require surgical removal. Consult your reptile veterinarian.

Respiratory Ailments

Because garter snakes and ribbon snakes have only a single functional lung, respiratory problems can quickly become fatal. The cause may be bacterial, viral, or even a parasite. A medication that works effectively on one species of snake might not work well on another. Some aminoglycoside drugs—which are ideally suited for curing a given respiratory problem—may be so nephrotoxic (dangerous to

A portrait of an orange colored eastern garter snake.

the kidneys) that they may kill the snake if the animal is at all dehydrated. Some bacteria are resistant to traditional antibiotics—ampicillin, amoxicillin, tetracycline, or penicillin. We suggest that you seek veterinary assessment of any respiratory problem. You can help by elevating the cage temperature (and sometimes by reducing the relative humidity). Quarantine the sick snake in a separate cage, preferably in a separate room.

Infectious Stomatitis (Mouth Rot)

An insidious and common disease, uncorrected mouth rot can result in permanent disfigurement, and perhaps in the death of your snake. Abrasions, a bite from a food rodent, mouth injuries, and unsanitary caging conditions cause this disease. It is characterized by areas of white, cheesy-looking exudate along the snake's gums. This material may be massive

enough to force the lips apart. Once the problem is detected, the mouth should be cleaned of the exudate. Use cotton swabs. Then wash the affected areas with hydrogen peroxide. Sulfa drugs (sulfamethazine seems to be the drug of choice) are effective against the bacteria that cause the disease. A veterinarian may suggest that you use

A portrait of the eastern ribbon snake, *T. s. sauritus*.

Although referred to as a Gulf Coast ribbon snake, those from near Brownsville, Texas have characteristics not entirely in keeping with that race.

Except for white lip and chin scales, many eastern garter snakes from near the Great Lakes are solid black.

an antibiotic as well. Complete eradication of mouth rot may take up to two weeks of daily treatment.

Blister Disease

If your garter snake develops tiny raised spots or nodules (these may be hard but are often suppurating) on its skin, an immediate assessment of cage conditions is in order. Blister disease is caused by the bacteria present when cages are very humid, damp, and/or dirty, or by soaking in unclean water. This is a potentially fatal disease.

The eastern ribbon snake is slender and precisely marked.

To eradicate this disease, change and improve your hygiene procedures.

If the blister disease is minimal, your snake probably will enter a "rapid shed cycle" and rid itself of the problems within a shed or two. If it is advanced with underlying tissue damage, your veterinarian may advise you to rupture each blister and clean the snake's skin daily. A dilute Betadyne and/or hydrogen peroxide solution may be used. Again, your snake will enter a rapid shed cycle and after a few sheds its skin should appear normal.

Endoparasites

Many reptiles, even those that are captive-bred and hatched, may harbor internal parasites. Today we are just beginning to realize the intricate role some parasites may play in the natural history of the snakes we keep, and that their presence in moderation may not be harmful. Because of the difficulties in identifying endoparasites, and the necessity to administer drug dosages by the weight of the snake, evaluation and possible eradication of internal parasites is best left to a qualified reptile veterinarian.

Colors

Of all the garter snakes, the eastern garter snake is known to be one of the most variable in coloration. There are three commonly seen color phases. The predominant phase is the familiar black ground color with three well defined yellow stripes. A second phase has a brownish ground color with weakly defined stripes and a strong checkerboard pattern on the sides. On the third phase, the yellow belly color extends upward on the sides to meet a variably defined checkerboard pattern on the upper sides. But there are many that are far from typical. Black individuals have been found, as have albinos. Several beautiful bright orange specimens have been seen in the eastern Carolinas; we found a greenish individual near Cincinnati, and recently photographed a brown individual with black stripes that was found in central Ohio.

Melanism and Albinism

Many species of garter snakes typically have a black ground color. However, occasionally, the black pigment suffuses even the light areas, or a form normally having an olive or brown body color may be largely or entirely black. Such prevalence of black pigment is termed melanism.

Melanism is not common. We have seen only a handful of melanistic Peninsula ribbon snakes, *T. sauritus sackenii*, from southwestern Florida, a single Baja garter snake, *T. validus celaeno*, from near La Paz, and a few eastern garter snakes, *T. s. sirtalis*, the race on which it is best documented.

The environs of Lake Erie—an area known for cool summer days, cold summer nights, and long, hard, winters—is a stronghold for a black phase of the eastern garter snake. On a recent trip to the region, we found

This magnificent ivory-white leucistic plains garter snake was owned and photographed by Paul Hollander.

This flame morph eastern garter snake is pretty, but not as spectacular as some. Photo by Phil Blais, M.D.

Albinism is well documented in eastern garter snakes. This example is from Massachusetts.

that the black phase actually predominated in some small areas, but was outnumbered by the striped phase in others nearby. The thought has been broached that perhaps black is a more efficient color for thermoregulation in this normally cool region. But if that were the case, it would seem that there would be fewer striped garter snakes there. There aren't enough data yet available to determine if the black phase is actually becoming more common.

Rather than the shiny black that we see on king and milk snakes, black garter snakes display a satiny luster. The belly may be slightly grayer than the back, and there are almost always a few white labial (lip) scales.

Although melanism has been reported from a few other species and subspecies of garter snake, it would appear that albinism—the absence of black pigment—is better known.

Amongst the garter snakes, albinism has cropped up in several species and subspecies. Albinos have been found in the before-mentioned eastern garter snake, the red-sided, *T. sirtalis parietalis*, the checkered, *T. m. marcianus*, and the Plains, *T. radix*. Albinos of all these are known.

A normally colored checkered garter is a pretty snake. The ground color is olive tan, the checkers (and neck-blotches) are black, and the stripes are cream to yellowish. Albino checkered garter snakes are even more beautiful. As juveniles, the checkers are pink to strawberry in color and appear almost translucent. The ground color is yellow-tan, and the stripes are somewhat lighter. As they

Until very recently the Baja garter snake, *T. validus,* was thought to be a water snake.

This very orange eastern garter snake, *T. s. sirtalis,* was seen in southeastern South Carolina.

grow, the snakes become lighter and lose their image of translucency, but are no less striking in color.

The normal coloration for the Plains garter snake is dark brown with two rows of black checkers between the yellow lateral and the orange vertebral stripes. When an albino, the ground color may be white to tan, the normally black checkers appear as squared, translucent, pinkish portholes, and the stripes are white. All in all, it is an interesting and pleasing combination of colors.

This all black peninsula ribbon snake was found in southwestern Florida.

New and Bright—The Flame (or Crimson) Morph of the Eastern Garter Snake

It had been a very long time since a new snake color morph got our attention. It began with the arrival of a new issue of a reptile hobbyist magazine. Once opened, three pictures accompanying an article almost leapt from the pages. The snake in the lead photo in the article was a stunner! It was predominantly red. And to me it seemed more crimson than flame. It was the color of a cardinal, a scarlet tanager, or a vermilion flycatcher—a beautiful, clear, absolutely eye-catching, bright red. It was even redder than the coveted (and federally endangered) San Francisco garter snake, the reddest natural form known. Meet the "new kid on the block" of color morphs, the flame, or crimson, garter snake.

The author of the article, Dr. Phil Blais, is a physician who lives near Montreal, Quebec. The snakes are the result of his linebreeding program in which he focused on a natural tendency toward redness that some of the garter snakes from his region had displayed.

The breeding program wasn't a one-season wonder; Dr. Blais has been working on it for almost half his lifetime. As a boy he acquired an eastern garter that had a red, rather than a yellow, lateral stripe. Eventually, he either found or was given one or two more. After a few years of selectively breeding the brightest with the brightest, his efforts began to pay off. But even once the babies are born, there's a delay factor built in. An extensive amount of ontogenetic (age-related) brightening occurs as the young mature. Even the duller neonates become red by the time they reach two years of age and shed several times.

Some of Dr. Blais' brighter stock has now been incorporated into the programs of breeders and their progeny are now entering the American pet trade. (We will be very interested in documenting the degree of ontogenetic color intensity that occurs in *our* specimens.)

Dr. Blais continues to linebreed his best specimens. What these garter snakes will look like after a few more generations of selective breeding can only be speculated upon, but if they get much brighter, you will need sunglasses to merely look at them!

This spectacular snake is one of Phil Blais' flame morph eastern garter snakes. Photo by Phil Blais, M.D.

Breeding

Sexing Snakes

Garter and ribbon snakes are easy to sex. Differences in the tail shape and tail length of sexually mature snakes allow visual sexing. The tail of a male is broader at the base than that of a similarly sized female. Also, the tail of the male usually tapers less abruptly and is comparatively longer. Other methods include probing, or by gently rolling your thumb along the bottom of a neonate's tail. (The latter will cause the hemipenes of a male to evert.)

Probing is the most reliable method of sexing all ages of garter and ribbon snakes. To be safe, the probe must be of the correct diameter—tiny for newborns and considerably larger for adults. When gently inserted into the hemipenial pocket of a male, a lubricated probe will slide smoothly back several subcaudal scale lengths further than it will in a female. Be careful—a probe that is too large or too small, or roughly used, can cause injury to the snake.

To evert the hemipenes of neonate males, place your thumb a few scales posterior to the vent and roll your thumb firmly, but very gently, forward. Females, of course, have no hemipenes to evert. This can only be done on a garter snake less than a month old; a snake older than this can be damaged by attempted eversion. Both visual sexing and manual eversion of the hemipenes is best learned from an experienced hobbyist.

Enhancing Reproductive Potential

Garter snakes bear living young. Normal litter size varies from 2 to about 20, but as many as 60 have been reported for the Plains garter snake, and 85 for the eastern garter snake. To put it mildly, when your female garter

Like garter snakes of all kinds, baby eastern black-necked garter snakes are slender and big-headed.

The northern ribbon snake, *T. sauritus septentrionalis,* occurs in southeastern Canada and U.S. border states.

gives birth, you'll have a number of very small babies, all instantly adept at escaping a cage that is escape-proof for their mother.

Breeding is most reliably accomplished if your garter snakes have been hibernated (the term brumated is often used for reptiles) for approximately three months during the winter. Where temperatures remain warm in winter, a refrigerator may need to be converted to a hibernaculum. An electrician can change the thermostat that controls the temperature in a refrigerator.

A garter snake may require a week after being removed from hibernation to warm up, wake up, and readjust to its surroundings before it chooses to feed. Others may feed almost immediately. Feed your snake heavily once it agrees to eat.

Mating may occur several times over several days. After mating behavior ceases, separate the sexes again. Continue feeding the snakes heavily. Your female should begin to gain weight, but even if heavily gravid, she may only look well-fed. If your female looks well-fed, assume she is gravid. Gestation is from 90 to 130 days. If after 2 to 3 months, your chubby female begins to refuse food, don't worry. Gravid females may refuse food for a week or two preceding parturition.

Another clue that your female is about to give birth is when she sheds. From 8 to 15 days prior to parturition, your female will shed her skin. This is your signal that "snake birth" soon will occur, and for you to finalize your plans on what you'll do with the babies. This is also the time to make certain the female's cage is escape-proof. Her water bowl should be shallow enough to allow the babies to escape, once they wander in. The lid of the cage should fit closely enough so that the babies, wet from the water bowl, can't take advantage of water adhesion and wriggle up the corners of the cage and through tiny gaps in the top. (It never occurred to me that baby garter snakes could or would do this, but when my grandmother found the babies in the hallway, it was obvious that something was up. I put the babies back in the cage and watched them try the technique again. Then I went out and bought another top.)

Following parturition, step up the feedings. It is best if your female snake quickly regains her body weight. Put the baby garters in their own cage, again to avoid problems with the now very hungry female. All the babies will fit comfortably in a 10- to 15-gallon (38- to 57-L) tank. Provide an absorbent substrate and a number of hiding areas, or use mulch/fallen leaves,

A litter of three neonate flame morph garter snakes. Photo by Phil Blais, M.D.

The Puget Sound garter snake, *T. sirtalis pickeringii,* is a dark race of western Washington and British Columbia.

Occasional examples of the red-spotted garter snake lack red.

which permit the babies to hide wherever they want. Provide a water dish, and expect the babies to spend part of their time in the water dish, soaking.

Like other baby snakes, the baby garters will *generally* refuse to eat until they've shed their skin. This is called the post-natal shed. Then they will slurp baby guppies out of their water bowl or swallow tiny earth-worms (or pieces of bigger earth-worms). Both foods are readily available from local bait or pet stores, or you may be able to dig earthworms and net tiny fish out of a local stream or pond (check to see if a license is necessary). Remember to feed the baby garters every other day or three times a week—they have a lot of growing to do—and increase the size of the food items as the babies themselves grow.

How to Hibernate Your Garter Snakes

Do not hibernate a snake that is thin or in otherwise suboptimal condition.

1. Stop feeding two weeks prior to cooling. Do not feed during the cooling period.
2. Place each snake in a separate hibernation receptacle. A covered plastic shoe box is fine.
3. Clear a shelf in a cool, little-used closet in a basement or garage for the hibernation cages. To hibernate successfully, snakes need temperatures between 45 and 56°F (7–13°C), minimal disturbance, and preferably continual darkness. (In the wild, a snake hibernates deep in a dark fissure, burrowed into a moist stump, or other similar humidity retaining area.)
4. Either a small dish of water should be kept in each hibernation container, or hibernating specimens should be roused for a drink every 15 days or so. If the snake does not drink, return it to its hibernation quarters and offer the water again in a week.
5. At the end of the hibernation period, simply put your snake in its regular caging.

Springtime Protocol

1. Remove the snake from hibernation, replace it in the cage, and provide a normal photoperiod.
2. Increase temperature to normal, between 85–95°F (29–35°C).
3. Increase relative humidity.
4. Begin offering food, and once the snakes are eating, feed them heavily.
5. When the snakes are fully active, and following the first post-hibernation shed (at this time pheromones indicate the snake's reproductive readiness), put the sexes together.
6. A gentle misting (simulating a rainstorm) may stimulate your snake's reproductive behavior. A simple spray bottle works fine. Aim it upward so the mist falls like a gentle rain.
7. If the snakes don't breed, place a second sexually mature male garter snake in the cage. The territoriality response often turns to reproductive interest.

Special Interest Groups

Herpetological Societies

Reptile and amphibian interest groups exist in the form of clubs, monthly magazines, and professional societies, in addition to herp expos.

Herpetological societies (or clubs) exist in major cities in North America, Europe, and other areas of the world. Most have monthly meetings, some publish newsletters, many host or sponsor field trips, picnics, or various other interactive functions. Information about these clubs can often be learned by querying pet shop employees, high school science teachers, university biology department professors, or curators or employees at the department of herpetology at local museums and zoos.

Two of the professional herpetological societies are:

Society for the Study of Amphibians
    and Reptiles (SSAR)
Dept. of Zoology
Miami University
Oxford, OH 45056

Herpetologist's League
c/o Texas National Heritage Program
Texas Parks and Wildlife Dept.
4200 Smith School Road
Austin, TX 78744

The SSAR publishes two quarterly journals. The *Herpetological Review* contains husbandry, range extensions, news on ongoing field studies, and so on, while the *Journal of Herpetology* contains articles more oriented toward academic herpetology.

Hobbyist magazines that publish articles on all aspects of herpetology and herpetoculture are:

Reptiles
P.O. Box 6050
Mission Viejo, CA 92690

Reptile and Amphibian Hobbyist
Third and Union Aves.
Neptune City, NJ 07753

The hobbyist magazines also carry classified ads and news about herp expos.

There are many excellent web sites that deal with reptiles and amphibians. Try:

www.Kingsnake.com Once the site is up, click on "forums," scroll down and click again on "garter and ribbon snakes." This site also lists herpetological societies and forthcoming expos, and posts a classified section.

www.PetPlace.com This is a good site especially for those new to the field. It has care articles for the most commonly kept reptiles and amphibians, as well as general information on caging, health, breeding, and feeding.

Glossary

Albino: Lacking black pigment.

Ambient temperature: The temperature of the surrounding environment.

Anterior: Toward the front.

Anus: The external opening of the cloaca; the vent.

Caudal: Pertaining to the tail.

cb/cb: Captive bred, captive born.

cb/ch: Captive bred, captive hatched.

Cloaca: The common chamber into which digestive, urinary, and reproductive systems empty and which itself opens exteriorly through the vent or anus.

Crepuscular: Active at dusk and/or dawn.

Dimorphic: A difference in form, build, or coloration involving the same species; often sex-linked.

Diurnal: Active in the daytime.

Dorsal: Pertaining to the back; upper surface.

Dorsolateral: Pertaining to the upper sides.

Ectothermic: "Cold-blooded," depending on external sources of warmth to raise the animal's body temperature.

Endemic: Confined to a specific region.

Endothermic: "Warm-blooded," the animal can control its body temperature without depending on external factors.

Form: An identifiable species or subspecies.

Genus: A taxonomic classification of a group of species having similar characteristics. The genus falls between the next higher designation of "family" and the next lower designation of "species." Genera is the plural of genus. It is always capitalized when written, like *Thamnophis*.

Gravid: The reptilian equivalent of mammalian pregnancy.

Hemipenes: The dual copulatory organs of male lizards and snakes.

Herpetoculture: The captive breeding of reptiles and amphibians.

Herpetology: The study (often scientifically oriented) of reptiles and amphibians.

Hibernacula: Winter dens.

Hybrid: Offspring resulting from the breeding of two species.

Intergrade: Offspring resulting from the breeding of two subspecies.

Jacobson's organs: Highly enervated olfactory pits in the palate of snakes and lizards.

Keel: A ridge (along the center of a scale).

Labial: Pertaining to the lips.

Lateral: Pertaining to the side.

Melanism: A profusion of black pigment.

Middorsal: Pertaining to the middle of the back.

A portrait of the red-spotted garter snake.

Midventral: Pertaining to the center of the belly or abdomen.

Monotypic: A taxonomic group (genus or species) containing only a single form.

Neonates: Newborns.

Nocturnal: Active at night.

Ontogenetic: Age related (color) changes.

Ovoviviparous: Reproducing by means of shelled or membrane-contained eggs that hatch prior to, or at deposition.

Parietal: Referring to the posterior most pair of enlarged scales on top of the head.

Photoperiod: The daily/seasonally variable length of the hours of daylight.

Postocular: To the rear of the eye.

Race: A subspecies.

Rostral: The (often modified) scale on the tip of the snout.

Scute: Scale.

Species: A group of similar creatures that produce viable young when breeding. The taxonomic designation that falls beneath genus and above subspecies. Always lowercase when written out. Abbreviation, "sp."

Subspecies: The subdivision of a species. A race that may differ slightly in color, size, scalation, or other criteria. Abbreviation, "ssp."

Sympatric: Occurring together.

Taxonomy: The science of classification of plants and animals.

Terrestrial: Land-dwelling.

Thermoregulate: To regulate (body) temperature by choosing a warmer or cooler environment.

Vent: The external opening of the cloaca; the anus.

Ventral: Pertaining to the undersurface or belly.

Ventrolateral: Pertaining to the sides of the venter (belly).

This is a blue-striped garter snake from Gulf Hammock, Florida.

Index

Availability—where to get, 14–18
Blister disease, 34
Breeding, 39–42
Caging, 19–26
  Cleaning, 20
  Furniture, 20
  Heating, 22
  Hides, 20–21
  Lighting, 22
  Plants 26
  Savanna Terrarium, 25–26
  Substrate, 20, 21, 25
Care—quick reference, 13, 19–29
Choosing your snake, 14
Clonophis kirtlandi, **6**
Feeding, 27–29
Handling, 13
Health, 30–34
Introduction, 3–4
Parasites, 31–32, 34
Purchasing, 16–18
Quarantine, 31
Respiratory distress, 32–33
Sexing, 39
Shedding, 30–31
Shipping, 17–18
Snake
  Garter
    Arizona, 10, **22**
    Baja, **4**, **37**
    Black-necked, 8–9
    Eastern, **8**, 8–9, **39**
    Western, **9**, 9
    Blue-striped, 6, **14**, **45**
    Butler's, 10, **11**, 31
    Checkered, 8, 9, **23**, **27**
    Chicago, 8
    Coastal, **4**, **7**, 10
    Eastern, 5, **13**, **17**, **21**, 24, 25, 26, 30, 32, 33, 34, 36, 37

Flame morph, **5**, **28**, **38**, 38, **42**
Maritime, 8
Narrow-headed, 9–10, **16**
New Mexico, 8
Northwestern, 10, **32**
Plains, **7**, 8, **35**
Puget Sound, 7, **42**
Red-sided, **7**, 7–8
  California, 8
Red-spotted, 8, **18**, **42**, **45**
San Francisco, **3**, 7, 15
Santa Cruz, 9, **10**
Short-headed, 10, **11**
Texas, 8
Two-striped, 9
Upper Basin, 10, **20**
Valley, 8
Wandering, 10, **19**
Kirtland's, **6**
Lined, **6**
Ribbon
  Aridland, 12, **21**, **22**
  Blue-striped, 12, **12**
  Eastern, 11, **33**, **34**
  Gulf Coast, 12, **29**, **33**
  Northern, 11, **40**
  Peninsula, **10**, 11–12, **37**
  Red-striped, 12, **12**
  Western, **2**, **4**, 12
Space requirements (see Caging)
Thamnophis
  atratus, 9, **10**
  brachystoma, 10, **11**
  butleri, 10, **11**, 31
  cyrtopsis, 8–9
    cyrtopsis, 9, 9
    ocellatus, **8**, 8–9, **39**
  elegans, 6, 10
    arizonae, 10, **22**
    terrestris, **4**, **7**, 10
    vagrans, 10, **19**

vascotanneri, 10, **20**
hammondi, 9
marcianus, 8–9
  marcianus, 8–9, **23**, **27**
ordinoides, 10, **32**
proximus, **2**, 11, 12
  diabolicus, 12, **21**, **22**
  orarius, 12, **29**, **33**
  proximus, **4**, 12
  rubrilineatus, 12, **12**
radix, 6, **7**, 8, **35**
rufipunctatus, 9–10, **16**
sauritus, 10, **11**–12
  nitae, 12, **12**
  sackenii, **10**, 11–12, **37**
  sauritus, 11, **33**, **34**
  septentrionalis, 11, **40**
sirtalis, 5–8
  annectens, 8
  concinnus, 6, **18**, **42**
  dorsalis, 8
  fitchi, 8
  infernalis, 8
  pallidulus, 8
  parietalis, **7**, 7–8
  pickeringii, 7, **42**
  semifasciatus, 8
  similis, 6, **14**, **45**
  sirtalis, 5, 5–6, **13**, **17**, **21**, **22**, **25**, **26**, **28**, **30**, **32**, **33**, **34**, **36**, **37**, **38**, 38, **42**, **45**
  tetrataenia, **3**, 7, 15
  validus, **4**, **37**
Tropidoclonion lineatum, **6**

Note: Page numbers in boldface type contain full-color photos.